# Beautiful
# San Diego

Concept and Design: Robert D. Shangle
Text: Loren Mitchell

Second Printing May, 1981
Published by Beautiful America Publishing Company
P.O. Box 608, Beaverton, Oregon 97075
Robert D. Shangle, Publisher

**Library of Congress Cataloging in Publication Data**
*Beautiful San Diego*
1. San Diego, Calif.—Description—Views. 1. Mitchell, Loren, 1930—
F869.S22M55   979.4'98   79-17663
ISBN 0-89802-060-3
ISBN 0-89802-059-X (paperback)

# Contents

Old San Diego . . . . . . . . . . . . . . . . . . . . . . . . . . . . . . . . 5

The City and the Suburbs . . . . . . . . . . . . . . . . . . . . . . 11

Within the City . . . . . . . . . . . . . . . . . . . . . . . . . . . . . . . 14

The Navy . . . . . . . . . . . . . . . . . . . . . . . . . . . . . . . . . . . . 67

The Park, The Zoo, and Watersports . . . . . . . . . . . . . 69

# Photo Credits

# Old San Diego

The miracle of San Diego is one of the great success stories of our time. People who have never visited the city might envision a sleepy border town surrounded by orange groves and the Pacific Ocean. Sailors who were stationed there might remember a small city, bathed in sunshine and inundated by thousands of Navy and Marine Corps personnel.

The reality of San Diego is something quite different. It is a major seaport, an industrial and electronics center, a year-around recreation area—and it's the ninth largest city in the United States. San Diego is bathed in sunshine most of the year, but the city's over-all climate is the important factor. San Diegans point out that their city owes its existence and its rapid growth to its nearly perfect weather, its large and protected harbor, and to the Spanish who founded the city and gave it its unique flavor and heritage.

All three elements become apparent to the visitor as he explores the city. He will admire the weather because it is seldom too hot or too cold. He will be drawn in fascination to Mission Bay and the busy harbor—the heart of the city—to watch boats and ships of all sizes come and go. He will seek out, photograph and inspect at close range every example of the city's background that he can find, from Mission San Diego de Alcala to the marvelous old victorian houses on Golden Hill.

From a contemporary point of view, one of the most startling things about San Diego is how long it took men to recognize the value of the city's fine harbor. Incredibly, more than 300 years elapsed between the discovery of the harbor and the first serious development that would put the harbor to use.

The story of San Diego properly begins in 1542, when Don Antonio de Mendoza, the first Viceroy of New Spain, commissioned Juan Rodriquez Cabrillo to command two tiny ships, the *San Salvador* and the *La Victoria* to explore the western side of California as far north as possible. It was not yet known if California was an island or part of a greater land mass, but the Viceroy ordered Cabrillo to "seek particularly rich lands" and to find the Straits of Anian—the fabled northwest passage.

Three months after leaving his home port of Navidad, Jalisco, Cabrillo sailed into San Diego Bay. He examined the shoreline, the sheltered bay, and the brown, treeless hills leading to the mountains in the distance, and claimed it all in the name of Carlos I, King of Spain. In his journal Cabrillo referred to his discovery, which he named San Miguel, as a ''very good sheltered port.'' Cabrillo died a few months later and was buried on one of the Santa Barbara Islands. His navigator, Bartolome Ferrelo took command of the expedition, returned home, and presented disappointed Spanish officials with Cabrillo's journals.

Concerned only in quick, tangible wealth, the Viceroy chose to ignore the discovery of the magnificent harbor and acted instead to develop trade with the Phillipines and China through the use of the ''Manila galleons''—the bulky trading ships that crossed the Pacific between New Spain and the Orient each year.

Spanish interest in *Alta California*—upper California—remained almost dormant for more than two centuries. When Sir Francis Drake anchored near San Francisco Bay in 1579, Spain reacted protectively and sent modest explorations up the California coast in 1584 and 1595. Don Sebastian Vizcaino embarked on a more thorough expedition in the summer of 1602, and that fall he located the bay at San Miguel and renamed it San Diego de Alcala in honor of the Spanish Franciscan friar whose holy day is November 13. On November 12, 1602, Carmelite friars who were travelling with Vizcaino celebrated mass on Point Loma—the first mass said in *Alta California*.

On his return to New Spain, Vizcaino delivered an enthusiastic report to the Viceroy and pointed out that the harbors he had seen would serve Spain well in her future expansion. Again, officials were not impressed and turned their energies to the settling of New Mexico rather than *Alta California*.

The decision to colonize California came slowly, and at first officials were primarily interested in *Baja*—lower—*California*. In 1697, the Jesuits received permission to begin a planned development in *Baja California*. One of their first enterprises was to establish a permanent colony and build a mission at Loreto, which was designed to be the mother mission for the entire mission system in California.

A threat from the Russians in the person of Vitus Bering finally prodded the Spanish authorities into colonizing *Alta California*. Bering had discovered and explored the Alaskan peninsula in 1734, and—still in no hurry—in 1766, Carlos III of Spain sent General Jose de Galvez as an emissary to oversee an expedition to *Alta California*. Captain Gaspar de Portola was to serve as the military leader, and Father Junipero Serra as the religious leader. Portola was to be governor of California, and

Father Serra, the president of the California missions. Their objective was to establish three missions and two presidios (forts) in *Alta California*. San Diego and Monterey were to receive both presidios and missions, and the third mission was to be built midway between the two sites at a still undetermined location.

After conferring with Galvez, Portola and Serra decided to take separate routes to San Diego. Portola would lead three ships loaded with tools, supplies and church goods while Serra would take a party overland, leading a herd of cattle which would be used as a food supply and serve to start the mission herds. Portola and Serra started their journeys in January, 1769. Portola's two ships—one had been lost at sea—arrived in San Diego in the middle of April, and Serra arrived on the first of July. The first mission and fort were constructed on a defensible hill above the south bank of the San Diego River, and on July 16—just two weeks after arriving, Father Serra dedicated his mission, which he named San Diego de Alcala.

Father Serra quickly discovered that his first mission was poorly located. Sharing the same hill with the presidio, it was too close to the soldiers and too far from the Indians that he hoped to convert. He selected a site for his permanent mission that was eight miles up the San Diego River. Six years after the first mission was built, Serra moved to the new and much larger mission. In November 1775, the Indians that Serra and his assistants had been working with revolted and burned the new mission, but the tireless Serra rebuilt the mission and dedicated it in 1780.

The object of the mission system, used by Spain throughout its new world frontiers, was to train native Indians to learn useful trades and to convert them from their ''savage'' state when they were called ''neophytes,'' to *gente de razon* or ''men of reason.'' This goal was to be accomplished with a minimum number of priests who hoped that the system would produce self-sufficient missions and a growing number of religious leaders from among the Indians, and that they would eventually be able to operate the missions by themselves.

The missions grew in size and number over the next 40 years. Mission San Diego de Alcala served as a base of operations for Portola and those who succeeded him as the area's military commanders. The mission also served as a supply source for each new mission, in all, 21, in a line that extended from San Diego to Sonoma. They were intentionally built about 30 miles apart so that each would be a comfortable day's ride from the other—undoubtedly for protection as well as convenience.

Mission San Diego de Alcala, like the other missions in *Alta California*, was intended to be a self-sufficient enterprise, but even when the mission system reached its peak in the 1820s few were self-sufficient for any length of time. Each mission owned thousands of acres of land and raised as much stock as the land could feed, but they were unable to provide many of the necessities of life. Missions were forced to trade hides—called "California Bank Notes" by the seamen whose ships stopped in San Diego, Santa Barbara and Monterey—for clothing, tools and furniture. A major cause of the failure of the mission system was the inability of the neophytes to adapt to the Spanish system. When they were removed from their native culture, they became listless and withdrawn.

It was inevitable that the mission system would fail, particularly after visitors to old California witnessed the plight of the mission Indians and often mistook their servitude for outright slavery. The end of the mission system came by surprise in 1833, when the 12-year-old Mexican government responded to public sentiment and removed them from Franciscan control, turning them over to a joint control of the mission Indians and the settlers in *Alta California*. Bewildered Indians and priests were forced into the background as settlers took charge of the mission holdings. Mission San Diego de Alcala quickly fell into ruins.

In his book, *Two Years Before The Mast*, Richard Henry Dana mentions that he visited the mission in San Diego in 1835, and found that it was already in decay. After California became a state, the United States Land Commission returned 22 acres of Mission San Diego de Alcala land to the Catholic Church, and the mission was rebuilt in 1931.

In 1835, when Dana first saw San Diego, he described "a chain of high hills, beginning at the point, protected the harbor on the north and west, and ran off into the interior as far as the eye could reach. On the other sides, the land was low, and green, but without trees." Dana also mentions that there was no town in sight—only four barn-like houses near Ballast Point used for storing hides. However, the town was there. It consisted of 35 or 40 buildings on the south side of the San Diego River, just below the hill that the mission and the old presidio had occupied—the site where Old Town is now. When Dana retraced his steps in 1859, he found the town of San Diego essentially unchanged—still a town with Mexican character.

The war with Mexico in 1846 through 1848 brought *Alta California* under the control of the United States. San Diego was incorporated in 1850, and California became a state in the same year. In that year, a man named William Heath Davis decided that San Diego had one of the finest harbors in the world and that someone should do something about it. He built a wharf and a warehouse near the foot of the present Market Street and encouraged Old Town residents to move into the area, which was about three miles south of where they had been living for years. A few did, but they moved quickly back to Old Town. It seems that the water supply in Davis' "New Town" was not only inadequate, but almost undrinkable! The wharf and the warehouse remained, but the new town was dubbed "Davis' Folly."

The concept of a new town being located on the waterfront was basically sound, however, and San Diego was forced to wait for a man to come along who had the money and leadership qualities necessary to turn the idea into reality. That man was Alonzo E. Horton who arrived from San Francisco on a boat in 1867. Like Davis, he saw that the town rightfully belonged where the ships came in. Horton bought 1,000 acres of brushy land near the wharf and laid out streets and building lots. He built a few houses to entice the population away from Old Town, but acceptance was understandably low. He finally guaranteed a good water supply and offered incentives to help the people move. They did, and San Diego began to grow.

Events during the next two decades favored the city's new location. It was incorporated again in 1872, and the city records were moved to a new location in Horton's development. The Santa Fe Railroad completed tracks from Los Angeles to San Diego in 1885, and as if to accent the changes, a fire swept through the wood frame houses in Old Town. At about the same time, two men named Babcock and Story bought the Coronado lands across the bay and began building what they promised to be one of the finest hotels in the western world. The Hotel del Coronado was finished in 1888, and instantly became an area landmark with a reputation for service for those who appreciated the good life. In the years that followed, Coronado continued to attract wealthy tourists, and many of those found the weather and scenery so agreeable that they built homes near the hotel.

By 1885, San Diego had a population of 3,000. In 1900, the city had grown to be a population of 17,700! In 1908, the San Diego Civic Improvement Committee—no doubt realizing that they were on the threshold of creating a fine city—hired the east coast architect and planner, John Nolen to redesign their city. Nolen studied their city, its topography and background, and presented the committee with a plan for a grand metropolis with broad boulevards edged with leafy trees, a wide parkway that stretched along the waterfront from Indian Point to Torrey Pines, civic buildings of Mediterranean architecture, and the development of Balboa Park.

Unfortunately, before Nolen's plans could be carried out, the citizens turned their attention to the financial gains that could be had in sponsoring a Panama-

California Exposition to celebrate the opening of the Panama Canal. Few of Nolen's concepts ever became reality, but his Mediterranean architecture was used for the exposition buildings along the El Prado in Balboa Park. The Panama-California Exposition did bring prosperity to the city. It opened in 1915, and San Diego's population swelled to 74,000!

From the turn of the century to the present, San Diego has experienced steady growth—due largely to its wonderful climate and excellent harbor. As recent as the 1950s much of Old Town was in a state of urban decay, with a few adobes serving as its only connection to the past. More recently, Old Town has been reclaimed with the colorful Bazaar del Mundo as the focal point. Outlying towns and farming communities such as El Cajon, La Mesa, Lemon Grove, National City and Escondido—most, once a part of the vast mission lands—have become a part of the metropolitan area. With a population approaching one million persons, San Diego continues to grow. One can't help wondering what Cabrillo, Vizcaino, or Portola might say if they were able to see their harbor today.

# The City
# And The Suburbs

Y ou learn about a watch by looking inside its case and closely examining its mechanism, but you can't learn about everything that way. Looking inside a city, for instance, will only tell part of the story. You have to observe the city in its setting; the surrounding ''bedroom'' communities, the nearby farms, and the mountain, lake or seashore recreation areas. All are part of the whole that gives a city its uniqueness.

So it is with San Diego—a city with an identity made up of small farming valleys in the north, the Mexican border and Tijuana in the south, sunny beaches and the Pacific Ocean on one side and mountains on the other. Within the city limits, San Diego spans almost 50 miles from north to south—from the rolling hills near Escondido to the Mexican border—and more than 20 miles from east to west, stopping just short of the mountains that separate the city from the desert country.

Geographically, the suburban land around San Diego varies from 70 miles of county and city-owned beaches to pine-covered mountains inland. Between the beaches and the mountains is a 20 to 30 mile-wide strip of semi-arid grass and brush-covered rolling hills and fertile valleys. Summer temperatures in San Diego range from warm along the coast—if the coastal fog has burned away—to hot inland. Evening temperatures are generally much cooler. Officially, the temperature average in San Diego is 68 degrees, and the annual rainfall figures about 11 inches, occuring in the first three months of the year.

Although the rainfall figures might seem too small, agriculture has been important to the economy of San Diego since the days of the mission system. The mission fathers began with cattle since they could be raised easily and hides were in great demand. Through the use of wells and irrigation, gardens and orchards were soon planted and to that extent the mission system was successful. Newcomers who arrived in San Diego in the last century quite likely threw up their hands in despair when they saw the dry hills around the little town, but must have rushed for land after seeing what could be grown on irrigated land.

Settlers established hundreds of small farms in the foothill valleys along the coast. As the numbers of small farms grew—their size was limited by the number of acres they could irrigate—and the population increased, farm towns began to appear. Vista, Escondido, Chula Vista, Lemon Grove, El Cajon, and La Mesa were among the first to be settled. Today, agriculture is still an important business in San Diego, ranking fourth in income after military, manufacturing and tourism. Principal crops are tomatoes, eggs, avocados, and nursery products. In fact, San Diego County is among the top 20 counties in the United States in agribusiness.

Some of the most visible evidence of San Diego's agribusiness is also the most beautiful. Motorists driving Interstate 5 near the beach cities of Carlsbad and Encinitas are favored with breathtaking views of the commercial flower farms along the east side of the highway. Look to the west and catch sunlighted vistas of the ocean.

By taking the old coast highway—now County Route S21—the coastal towns can be toured at the leisure pace that they deserve, and there is plenty to see! Almost every beach city has interesting boutiques and gift shops, good beaches—Encinitas claims the safest in the state—and seafood restaurants. Carlsbad's Alt Karlsbad Hanse House gift shop is built over a mineral spring, and the water has the reputation of being similar to the waters in Karlsbad, Czechoslovakia.

Farther south, Coronado is another beach city that is not a part of San Diego's city limits. Coronado, together with the North Island Naval Air Station, is actually the tip of a seven-mile-long narrow peninsula called the Silver Strand. Travel between Coronado and San Diego had been limited to a mile-long ferry ride until recently when a bridge was opened between the two cities. The focus of Coronado remains the Hotel del Coronado. Known locally as the ''del,'' the sprawling old hotel with its carefully manicured flower gardens, green lawns, and picturesque palm trees is a national historical landmark.

The long beaches on the Silver Strand stretch away to the south, toward Imperial Beach, the Mexican Border and Tijuana. Each year visitors arrive in San Diego believing that the nearest large city is Los Angeles, yet Tijuana is only 18 miles from San Diego and has a population of three-quarters of a million people—equal in size to San Diego. The nearness of Tijuana gives recreation in the San Diego area an added dimension and tints the entire region with an ambience of Mexican culture. While the flavor of Old Mexico still exists throughout San Diego, one only has to cross the border for the real thing. Aside from the ever-present gift and curio shops in Tijuana, there is the opportunity to see Jai-alai at the Fronton Palace, horse racing at Agua Caliente Race Track, or see a bullfight in Tijuana's bull ring.

The small communities that separate east San Diego from the Mountains may lack the color of Tijuana, but their importance to the city is indisputable. El Cajon, La Mesa, and Lemon Grove, like the more southerly cities of Chula Vista and National City, are a part of San Diego in every respect, except that they are completely autonomous. To a stranger, the borders of these cities merge so thoroughly that they appear to be parts of the same city. Most are home communities for San Diego, but they also have their own reasons for existing. National City and Chula Vista have an economic base of aerospace, electronics, and manufacturing plants. National City has the largest port facilities in the area, and shares a Navy base with San Diego. Lemon Grove was the location of some of the most fertile mission lands and because of the climate, truck gardens in the area still produce three or four crops a year.

Agriculture, however, appears to be a diminishing part of the suburban scene in San Diego. Farm and grazing lands once surrounded the carefully groomed, sun-bathed communities of Rancho Santa Fe and San Marcos—both in the North County—where harried executives could come for a few quiet days of golf and relaxation. Now, both towns, as well as others in the area feel the encroachment of planned communities, housing tracts, and industrial parks. With development land selling at a premium closer to downtown San Diego, the bulk of the new housing is being planned along the low rolling hills as far north as Carlsbad and Escondido.

On the positive side, farms beyond metropolitan San Diego still contribute to the city's economy, and suburban homes—particularly in San Diego's clean air environment—provide an open air, healthy situation that is ideal for family living. The proximity of the mountains, the beaches, the cities, and the border enhance the excitement of being in San Diego.

# Within The City

There's a very old joke that comedians like to use to make a point. In describing San Diego they might say something like, "San Diego has a perfect climate, a beautiful natural harbor, a perfect climate, all kinds of water sports, a perfect climate, economic vitality, a perfect climate, etc." In short, San Diego is a dynamic city.

Any San Diegan—most likely a native of one of the mid-western or eastern states—will gesture toward new houses with verdant lawns or high-rise buildings with tinted glass facades, talk about the climate, then tell you about the job he sacrificed to move west. Then, the conversation will turn to the fuel bills, the winter clothing, the tire chains, and other headaches about the winters where he came from—which he doesn't miss—and tell you more about San Diego. It's a story everyone has heard. Even the most recent new citizen of the city is thankful that he had the wisdom and the courage to make the move. After all, even the most out-spoken doubter will agree that there has to be a reason why San Diego has tripled its population since World War II!

San Diego hasn't experienced its rapid growth without careful, thoughtful plan-ning. The older, established neighborhoods like Sherman Heights and Golden Hill—both just east of the city center—have not lost their identities. Several dozen elegant old Victorian houses have been restored to their former elaborate attrac-tiveness for the public to view. However, many of the homes are private residences or have been converted to private professional offices and are not open for public tours.

Lovers of Victorian architecture will want to see Heritage Park in Old Town. Save Our Heritage Organization (SOHO) is the agency responsible for relocating the stately houses, displaced by new construction, to a hillside setting of lawns, flower beds and walkways that is reminscent of life a century ago.

Since Old Town is the oldest neighborhood in San Diego, it follows that it has seen the most changes. A scant 25 years ago, Old Town was a problem area. A few adobes were all that remained of the Spanish and Mexican eras, and the district had been built over with nondescript houses and small business buildings. Since then, the area has been resurrected through careful commercial development to provide visitors with an interesting and colorful approximation of the Mexican way of life in early San Diego. In its six block area are El Camp Santo, a cemetery that dates back to the 1850s; Bazaar del Mundo, a Mediterranean-style cluster of shops and restaurants set around a central garden; Plaza Vieja, the original Old Town plaza; and a dozen-odd homes and buildings of the Mexican era. If you want to see Old Town in high style, hire the horse and buggy at the park headquarters on Wallace Street.

The site of the original presidio and Father Serra's first mission are at the top of the hill directly east of Old Town. The hill top is now called Presidio Park and the Serra Museum stands where the mission and presidio once stood. The Serra Museum, named in honor of Father Junipero Serra, houses an excellent collection of artifacts from the Spanish and Mexican periods of old California.

Once atop Presidio Hill, one realizes that the hill is really a point of land extending from the plateau to the east. From Presidio Hill, a bee-line eastward would carry you through the established San Diego districts of Mission Hills, Hillcrest, North Park, Normal Heights, and the Montezuma area near San Diego State University. While a ''bee-line'' might seem to be a fanciful concept, a real bee-line through the area exists in the form of El Cajon Boulevard and Washington Street. These two east-west main arterials combine in their length to form a thoroughfare that stretches from San Diego International Airport on the bay, up through Mission Hills—a district of fine older homes—and eastward across the plateau to El Cajon. Washington Street begins at the airport and meets El Cajon Boulevard in the middle-class district of North Park. Busy, bustling El Cajon Boulevard remains essentially unchanged since the early years following World War II when it was the backbone of the city with its car lots, fast food restaurants, and myriad of small businesses.

1,400-acre Balboa Park is located between North Park and the downtown district. The vast park serves as a sanctuary for busy San Diegans who regularly play on the park's 18 hole municipal golf course, visit the zoo to watch animals and birds in a near-natural habitat, take part in the cultural activities along the El Prado, or just relax under a tall eucalyptus tree near 6th Avenue. The busy activity in the city center below the park, and in the bay beyond, can be quickly forgotten in the serenity of the huge park. Despite the fact that high-rise apartment buildings going up along 6th Avenue are beginning to block views of the bay, and Point Loma across the bay, one can still find a quiet spot in the park from which to enjoy the view.

Point Loma stands like a guardian over the mouth of San Diego Bay. Its land mass runs north and south, extending five miles from the mouth of the San Diego

River channel southward to the high promontory at the point effectively sheltering the mouth of San Diego Bay from the sea. From atop the point where an old decommissioned lighthouse and the Cabrillo National Monument are, one can look across the bay waters and the Naval Air Station and see the five miles distant city and the trees of Balboa Park.

Point Loma is an area that is almost isolated from the mainstream of activity in San Diego. Like the point of an inverted hook, it is separated from its base by the airport, the Navy and Marine Corps training centers, the waters of San Diego Bay, and to the north the mouth of the San Diego River and Mission Bay. Loma Portal, a large district on the east side of Point Loma was originally settled by Italian, Sicilian, and Portugese families who established the tuna fishing industry in San Diego. Originally a neighborhood with a colorful ethnic character, Loma Portal has grown and blended with the times, producing a well-kept district of attractive homes. Ocean Beach is situated on the west side of Point Loma, and is a quiet community with lovely homes that overlook Sunset Cliffs and the Pacific Ocean. Ocean Beach has the longest fishing pier on the Pacific Coast.

Vizcaino mentioned in his journals that San Diego had a false bay—a bay just north of Point Loma—that had a large tidal basin and was fed by a river. He was talking about Mission Bay, and for the past 20 years San Diego has been working on an expensive $60 million program reclaiming the tidal lands of the bay to convert the entire area into a 4,600-acre aquatic park. Mission Bay is a water playground with marinas, resort hotels, restaurants, and Sea World—an 80-acre marine-life park.

Mission Bay was once considered the domain of the Mission Beach district, a narrow densely-built neighborhood located on a two-mile long strip of land that separates Mission Bay from the ocean. Ocean Front Walk, a concrete promenade that parallels the beach, was once a place to stroll, munch hot dogs, and eat candied apples. People still enjoy the promenade, but nowadays they're riding skateboards and roller skates.

A few miles north of Mission Beach lies the attractive beach community of La Jolla. Its name in Spanish is taken from the word for "jewel"—a name well-suited to the location. La Jolla is located on a broad point of land that is dotted with small beaches and rocky outcroppings. Large homes, unusual apartment buildings, and picturesque hotels have been built along the shoreline, giving the area a distinctive atmosphere. Farther north, the buildings of Scripps Institute and the University of California at San Diego, and the long sandy beach and cliffs below Torrey Pines

*Flamingos at the San Diego Zoo*

*Sea World Tower*
*(Following pages) San Diego waterfront*

*Coronado Bay Bridge, from Coronado*
*(Following pages) Bazaar Del Mundo, Old Town*

*Hotel del Coronado*

23

*La Jolla shoreline*

*Lions, San Diego Zoo*

*Oceanside: Marina and whaling village*

*The Serra Museum in Presidio Park*

*Sunset Cliffs*

*Fort Rosecrans National Cemetery*

31

*Pacific Beach*

*Mission tower*

Torrey Pines Beach
(Following pages) Shelter Island, city skyline from Pt. Loma

Ranunculus flowers in north San Diego County

35

*Ranch and orange groves, north San Diego County*

*Street scene*
*(Following pages) La Jolla in the springtime*

La Jolla

Old Town Courtyard

*San Diego skyline from Harbor Island*

*Balboa Park*

*The Immaculata, University of San Diego campus*

*Sailboats at anchor, Ventura Bridge in background*

*City skyline from harbor*

*Mission San Diego de Alcala*

*Downtown San Diego with the U.S. Grant Hotel*
*(Following pages) Botanical Garden, Balboa Park*

*Japanese Bell of Friendship*

*An orange grove near San Diego*

*Old Town Courtyard*
*(Following pages) San Diego skyline from Coronado*

*La Jolla from Mt. Soledad*

*Santa Fe Railroad Station*

59

*Tuna boats in port*

*Torrey Pines State Park*

*Cliffs overlooking the Pacific*

*San Diego skyline from Golden Hills Drive*

dominate the scene. On weekends you can watch hang-glider enthusiasts sail off the cliffs and land on the beach 400 feet below.

Over the centuries, the San Diego River—as small as it is—carved out Mission Valley, from the foothills near El Cajon to the point where the river flows into the ocean between Point Loma and La Jolla. Mission Valley acts as a natural division between the older, more established southern half of the city and the more modern housing tracts and shopping centers in the north. From the days of the Spaniards until recently, the fertile bottom land in the mile-wide valley was used almost exclusively for farming. Because of the growth San Diego has experienced, the valley land has been developed into golf courses, shopping centers, hotels and motels, and the San Diego Stadium.

As one might expect of a city the size of San Diego, professional sports is well-represented, and the teams have a lot of fans. San Diego is the home of the pro-football Chargers and the pro-basketball Clippers. In professional baseball, soccer, and hockey, the teams are the Padres, the Sockers, and the Hawks, respectively. Indoor sports are enthusiastically followed in the Sports Arena which is located a mile west of Old Town near Mission Bay.

To mention sports in San Diego without considering golf would be a grave error. With a nearly perfect year-around climate, it is to be expected that San Diego would be called ''Golfland U.S.A.'' There are 67 golf courses in the county—half of them within San Diego's city limits—giving the city more golf courses per capita than any other metropolitan area in the world. Only 19 of the courses are private, giving the San Diego visitor plenty of challenging play.

Sports isn't the only aspect of culture represented in San Diego, however. The city has an active cultural base in art museums, natural history museums, legitimate theater, opera, ballet and a symphony orchestra. The city's annual Shakespearian Festival presented in Balboa Park's Globe Theater is world-renowned.

The pursuit of culture can be had in more formal ways, too. Higher education in San Diego is available through six accredited four-year colleges and universities. School of Law are offered at the University of San Diego, Western State University, and the California Western School of Law. The University of California at San Diego has a medical school at the Scripps Institute of Oceanography. In addition, nine community college campuses serve the city and county areas.

In the past 20 years, San Diego has grown from the economically precarious position of being a one-industry city to that of economic diversity. By actively seeking

*Pt. Loma Lighthouse*

out low polluting, desirable industries such as electronics, research and development, and computer-oriented business, San Diego has been able to display remarkable growth. The result is high-rise buildings going up in the city center, a community concourse to house city offices, and restoration projects like the Gaslamp Quarter, Seaport Village, and the waterfront Embarcadero project. The city limits have reached northward to the boundaries of Escondido, and to include the communities of Mira Mesa, Rancho Bernardo, and the Wild Animal Park near San Pasqual.

No visit to San Diego should be attempted without endeavoring to see it all—the beaches, Balboa Park, La Jolla, Coronado, the Wild Animal Park—and an excellent way to do it is to take one of the many tours that serve the area, or follow the 52-mile self-guiding auto tour. It includes most of the points of interest in this beautiful city.

# The Navy

To most San Diegans, the Navy is as much a part of the city as the zoo is of Balboa Park. The Navy connection has been here almost forever, and it would be hard to imagine the city without it. However much of that reasoning may seem to be "tunnel vision," the people of San Diego can rightfully lay claim to the existence of the strong military presence. And it is no accident that the city encouraged the Navy to build bases along its waterfront during the years between World Wars I and II, banking on the hope that someday the Navy would help bring economic stability.

The gamble has paid off handsomely. At the present time, the Navy adds $1.5 billion annually to the economy of San Diego. Every third worker in San Diego County is employed by the Navy in some capacity, and one-fourth of the county population is Navy—including civilian employees, military personnel, dependents, and retired Navy people.

Of course, the decision to establish military bases in San Diego wasn't a selfless act on the part of the Navy. From the day when the U.S.S. Alert entered San Diego Bay in 1842, and prematurely sent men ashore to capture the town—under the mistaken belief that the United States and Mexico were already at war—the Navy has been interested in San Diego. Agreeing with Juan Cabrillo, many Navy officials call San Diego a very good port. Others go further by calling it the best naval anchorage in the world. All are in agreement that San Diego's climate makes it an ideal place for a training center.

After sailors from the U.S.S. Cyane, under the command of Captain Samuel DuPont, raised the first American flag over the tiny presidio on the hill above Old Town in 1846, the Navy presence in San Diego began to grow. At first it was limited to occasional visiting ships until the government bought land on Point Loma and established a coaling station there in 1901. In 1906, the Navy built a radio station and in 1940 added the Naval Electronics Laboratory. The old radio station was decommissioned in 1949, when the Navy Communications Center was established near Imperial Beach.

North Island Naval Air Station is especially significant in naval history. When the Hotel del Coronado opened in 1888, North Island was almost totally separated from Coronado by an inlet called Spanish Bight. The island was little more than high land at the time, connected to Coronado by a narrow strip of sand. The Navy decided that North Island was a perfect place to work with Glenn Curtiss in 1911, in proving the feasibility of landing aircraft on and near ships. In doing so, North Island became a birthplace of naval aviation.

In 1914, North Island became home for the Fourth Marine Regiment, and the Army began to develop an airfield there that they called Rockwell Field. The start of World War I in Europe sparked a military consciousness in the United States, and in 1917, the Navy was given funds to take over Curtiss' old buildings on the island and build a permanent installation. By the time Charles Lindbergh took off from North Island in 1927, on the first leg of his record-breaking flight in the *Spirit of St. Louis* (a San Diego-built plane), Spanish Bight had been filled in and the Navy air station was in operation.

The Navy had started the amphibious base, auxiliary airfields in the county, an ammunition depot near Fallbrook, and the Navy station on Harbor Drive before 1920. In the next five years San Diego became the headquarters of the Eleventh Naval District, the Navy-commissioned hospital, a supply depot, and the Navy and Marine Corps training bases. The first Naval Training Center was established in 1917 in San Diego, using the old Panama-California Exposition buildings in Balboa Park. After a frenzy of construction around both sides of the harbor, the Navy emerged well-established in San Diego with scores of new arcaded stucco buildings that hundreds of thousands of men would ultimately serve duty in.

As a result of the goodwill that has been established between the military and the people of San Diego, there has been a long-standing invitation for civilians to visit Navy installations on special occasions. For instance, the public is invited to watch Navy ''boots'' go through close order drills and marching each Saturday at the Naval Training Center, to watch Marine recruits do the same thing on Fridays at the neighboring Marine Corps Recruit Depot, and to visit Navy ships each weekend at Harbor Drive and Broadway. In case anyone should wonder if the public is interested in all this military exposure, air shows at the huge Miramar Naval Air Station—located a dozen miles north of San Diego—have drawn as many as 300,000 persons.

Ask any ex-sailor if he has ever been to San Diego. The chances are he has, and has fond memories of a very nice city.

# The Park, The Zoo, and Watersports

## Balboa Park and The Zoo

Aside from the climate, most visitors are drawn to San Diego to see Balboa Park and the San Diego Zoo. San Diegans are indebted to the city's founders for the park, for in 1868, they exercised the unusual foresight in setting aside 1,400 acres of hilltop land to be a public park forever. In those early years of the city's history, funds were not available to develop the park and the land was virtually unused for more than 20 years.

Finally a horticulturist named Kate Sessions came to an agreement with the city to begin developing the park land. In exchange for the use of a few acres of the park for a nursery, she agreed to plant flowers and shrubbery at the park entrance. Her magnificent efforts were not forgotten, for after the turn of the century a community action program was started to develop the park by citizens who were inspired by Mrs. Session's work.

At about the same time, merchants in San Diego began to realize that expositions were good business, and after some discussion, saw a way to develop the city *and* the park. The people of the small city decided to tax their economy to the limit and hold an elaborate fair in honor of the completion of the Panama Canal. When President Woodrow Wilson opened the Panama-California Exposition on January 1, 1915, the population of San Diego doubled. During the year, the exposition attracted over 3 million persons.

The only permanent building constructed for the exposition was the California Building which houses the Museum of Man. Its ornate California Tower and tiled dome can be seen from all around the park. Only a few of the temporary buildings remain today. Some have burned and others have been torn down and replaced by permanent structures.

A second exposition in 1935—the California-Pacific International Exposition—provided the motivation to restore the aging exposition buildings, and to build a few more. The Spanish Village and the Old Globe Theater were built for the 1935 exposition. The Old Globe Theater was a copy of the London theater of the same name and was the home of San Diego's famed Shakespeare Festival. (The Old Globe Theater and the Aerospace Museum were recently destroyed by fire, but are currently being rebuilt).

A walk down El Prado, the main street through the park that leads from Cabrillo Bridge, will reveal the wonders and beauty of Balboa Park. Aside from the Museum of Man, other points of interest are the Fine Arts Gallery and the Timken Gallery, which have permanent collections from most periods in art history. Here one can view masterworks by Titian, Goya, Velasquez, Rubens, and Rembrandt.

The House of Charm has a large model railroad layout, which is open to the public on Sundays, a sports museum, and exhibits by the San Diego Art Institute. The Botanical Building houses hundreds of varieties of plants, and the Natural History Museum has a fascinating array of fossils, and mounted birds and animals.

The area south of El Prado has the Spreckels Outdoor Organ Pavilion, where free concerts have been presented almost every Sunday afternoon since 1915. The Starlight Bowl, located near the Organ Pavilion, has been the location of thousands of outdoor symphony concerts, plays, operas, and musical presentations. Across the road from the Spreckels organ, the House of Pacific Relations—really a cluster of cottages—holds an open house with people of a different nationality each Sunday.

El Prado ends at a large, round flowing fountain. The Casa del Prado is nearby, and the Spanish Village—a center for working artists—is a block or two north. El Prado is less than a mile long, yet it gives Balboa Park a uniqueness that no other city park in the United States can claim.

By anyone's estimation, the San Diego Zoo is one of the finest in the world. It began in 1916, when Dr. Harry Wegeforth gathered animals that had been on display at the Panama-California Exposition and placed them on public display in pens that had been built in the rugged canyons on the north side of Balboa Park. Concerned citizens gave him financial support until the zoo was brought under city control in 1934.

Since 1934, the zoo has grown to a 128-acre subtropical garden-like home for 5,500 animals, representing over 1,600 species. An outstanding feature of the zoo is that wherever possible, the animals have been placed in roomy pens that closely match their native environments. Huge aviaries rising above the tree tops contain an amazing variety of birds. The zoo may be seen by walking through it, by taking a slow-moving open air bus, or by taking the Skyfari—an aerial lift that travels above the zoo.

As one might expect, Balboa Park also has the anticipated park features like tennis courts, a swimming pool, a velodrome, a golf course, and athletic fields—all in the eastern half of the park.

# A Watersports Vacationland

Take a drive to Point Loma, out Catalina Boulevard to the Cabrillo National Monument. Facing east, San Diego Bay starts below and sweeps north around North Island, then bends around to the southeast to almost disappear in the distant haze. If you stand there for a while and watch the activity on the water below, with the statue of Cabrillo by your side, you can't miss being a witness to San Diego's most popular outdoor activity—boating.

Navy warships and cargo ships come and go, but mixed in with all the commercial and military water activity will be dozens of pleasure boats of all kinds. They travel from marinas on Coronado, Harbor Island, and Shelter Island, sailboats leaning with the wind while power boats speed in and out, soon leaving the slower craft behind. It's a relaxing activity that San Diegans love, and proof of this claim can be had by visiting the bay any warm weekend when hundreds of small boats seem to crowd the waters.

Passive outdoor enthusiasts may be content to visit the Maritime Museum on the Embarcadero, between Broadway and Ash Streets, and board the 1863 vintage *Star of India*, or take the one or two-hour harbor excursion tour. Nearby, tuna fishermen can be seen in the almost daily task of mending their nets.

Mission Bay Aquatic Park actually has 27 miles of shoreline and 2,500 acres of water that is devoted to aquatic sports. Private firms on both bays offer pedal craft, kayaks, cat boats, pontoon barges, sailboats, and motor boats for hire.

Deep-sea fishermen can take party boats from landings in Oceanside, Imperial Beach, San Diego, and Mission Bay. Permits are not required when fishing from commercial sportfishing boats, but inquiries can be made about licenses at the California Department of Fish and Game, and the Mexican Fish Commission offices in San Diego.

Skin-diving enthusiasts will find good diving off Sunset Cliffs and La Jolla. Lobster, abalone, and big game fish are plentiful in season.

# Beautiful America Publishing Company

*The nation's foremost publisher of quality color photography*

## Current Books

Alaska
Arizona
Boston
British Columbia
California
California Vol. II
California Coast
California Desert
California Missions
California Mountains
Chicago
Colorado
Dallas
Delaware
Denver
Florida
Georgia
Hawaii
Idaho
Illinois
Indiana
Kentucky
Las Vegas
Los Angeles, 200 Years

Maryland
Massachusetts
Michigan
Michigan Vol. II
Minnesota
Missouri
Montana
Montana Vol. II
Monterey Peninsula
Mormon
Mt. Hood (Oregon)
Nevada
New Jersey
New Mexico
New York
New York City
Northern California
Northern California Vol. II
North Carolina
North Idaho
Ohio
Oklahoma
Orange County
Oregon

Oregon Vol. II
Oregon Coast
Oregon Country
Pacific Coast
Pennsylvania
Pittsburgh
San Diego
San Francisco
San Juan Islands
Seattle
Tennessee
Texas
Utah
Utah Country
Vancouver U.S.A.
Vermont
Virginia
Volcano Mt. St. Helens
Washington
Washington Vol. II
Washington, D.C.
Wisconsin
Wyoming
Yosemite National Park

## Forthcoming Books

Alabama
Arkansas
Baltimore
Connecticut
Detroit
The Great Lakes
Houston
Kansas

Kauai
Maine
Maui
Mississippi
New England
New Hampshire
North Dakota

Oahu
Phoenix
Rhode Island
Rocky Mountains
South Carolina
South Dakota
West Virginia

## Large Format, Hardbound Books

Beautiful America
Beauty of California
Beauty of Oregon

Beauty of Washington
Glory of Nature's Form

Lewis & Clark Country
Western Impressions